Velvet Passions

of

Calibrated Quarks

Caroline Nazareno-Gabis

inner child press, ltd.

Credits

Author
Caroline Nazareno-Gabis

Foreword
Eunice Barbara C. Novio

Cover Design
Inner Child Press, ltd.

~ * ~

In an attempt to preserve the author's authentic voice, the content of the original poetry submission has not been edited for this compilation.

hülya n. yılmaz, Ph.D.
Director of Editing Services

General Information

Velvet Passions of Calibrated Quarks
Author: Caroline Nazareno-Gabis

1st Edition: 2020

This publishing is protected under Copyright Law as a "Collection". All rights for all submissions are retained by the individual author and / or artist. No part of this publishing may be reproduced, transferred in any manner without the prior **WRITTEN CONSENT** of the "Material Owner" or its representative Inner Child Press, ltd. Any such violation infringes upon the creative and intellectual property of the owner pursuant to International and Federal Copyright Law. Any queries pertaining to this "Collection" should be addressed to Publisher of Record.

Publisher Information
1st Edition: Inner Child Press
intouch@innerchildpress.com
www.innerchildpress.com

This Collection is protected under U.S. and International Copyright Laws

Copyright © 2020: Caroline Nazareno-Gabis

ISBN-13: 978-1-952081-02-6 (inner child press, ltd.)

$ 8.95

Dedication

To my parents, Camilo and Aurora
who are now with our Creator,

To my loving husband, Bryann
and to the baby in my womb,

To my wonderful friends, my Poetry Posse
family, peacemakers and educators, readers
and those who in one way or the other
supported me to make this book possible

Table of Contents

Preface ix

Foreword xi

The Poetry

Biography of a Face	3
Biography of a Spirit	4
Nirvana in Your Rainbow	5
Interstice	6
Whipping Prophesy	7
Mother, There's No Other	8
The Verge	9
River of Golden Intaglio	10
soon-to-be-sun poetry	11
Euphoria 10.16.17	12
Wish	13
Devi's Mundial De Tango	14
The Song My Heart Sings	15
Euphoric Diffusion	16

Table of Contents... *continued*

Where Peace Can Be	17
Waltz With the Rain Princess	18
Sequester X	19
Nexus in My Canvas	20
Meraki	22
Call Me Cypher	23
Bedazzled	24
because i can be	25
I See No Other from Yesterday	27
Pandora escapes unto my hands	28
Godiva and the Music	29

Epilogue — 31

About the Author	33
Author's Links	35

Preface

Feel and fall!

Then, be filled in the vacuum of rhythmic particles!

Velvet Passions of Calibrated Quarks is a collection of twenty-five poems from different seasons of my monumental saga. It is my life-story in manifolds; a record of my vivid, dynamic and groundbreaking introspection as I sing, dance and fly! A fusion and diffusion of my honeyed confessions, which were written from and for my real encounters, experiences, favourite places, and events— the quintessence of my inner-self through poetic innovation and evolution. Some of which I had already performed in the international festivals of arts, poetry and literature.

I formulate a chef-d'œuvre by putting a heart, mind and soul. When I write poetry, I gain more inspiration. My humble poetic offerings become a fireball, up to speed; an aubade to the rigmaroles reverberating in my odyssey. I believe that the creative spirit in us will be a kiss of metamorphosis; an influential radiance of Cosmos; and a reminder of becoming the best and the great ones betwixt the vacuum of diversity.

Poetry is a powerful tool that inspires, motivates, encourages, uplifts, and becomes our language. It does not cease to create a spark of change for the individuality and humanity. It is like a special space of atomic molecules of everyday life; an aroma that sticks in your nose; an anaesthetic balm that makes wounds or pain disappear, and like a neuro booster that refills the human consciousness.

This book simply defines the epitome of life and love – that transmogrifies the tiniest dream to a reality, rebuilt with miracles and wisdom beyond metaphors.

Thank you for shaping me to be a better woman.

Caroline Nazareno-Gabis

Foreword

I have been reading Caroline Nazareno or Ceri Naz in the literary circle since 2010 when she accepted me as a friend on Facebook. I thought she was one of the many aspiring poets who would one day wane in their words and rhythms as years passed. I have known many of these kinds of poets and writers, but Ceri Naz proved me wrong.

The diversity of her poetry makes her 'award-winning'. For me, she has developed another genre, which is *diversified poetry*. Her poems are about women and human empowerment, love, sacrifice, self-rediscovery, friendship, peace, New World, cosmos and science.

Her poetry is lyrical. Her words are full of imageries that linger in your memory. Her poetry entertains, enchants and moves you into deep thoughts.

The poetry of Ceri Naz reflects her empowerment as a woman and as an individual. Her poetry is like her; a dreamer, a believer, always looking for new things even reaching the cosmos and Mars. For her, infinite is the only definite.

Ceri Naz is a poet for the human race.

Eunice Barbara C. Novio

Journalist, Author, Educator
Women's Advocate

The Poetry

Caroline Nazareno-Gabis

Velvet Passions of Calibrated Quarks

Biography of a Face

I see her standing in front of the mirror
Striking her hair in fishtail
The moment she puts on a lipstick
She thinks she have just painted
Another story for a brand-new day
It adds color and sassy look
She models her scarlet veil and her crimson doll shoes
She likes the way her cup B sized bras are kept
With tags of memories of battling the battles within her battles
It is like her cry conquers the rhythms of liberty
Garlands of hope reverberate in back to back trends
Of surviving the daily wars inside and outside
She makes her oncologist feel
She can stand, and be back on her mountaineering
Her force is beyond a millionaire's wish
Just like her, the host of outnumbered dreams
Another life in joining miracles
When one-roofed litanies of women warriors
Trying to save the clans of goodwill and heralds of compassion
The milestone has just defined the voiceless
From the selfless
Even the yellow and pink ribbons could praise
The wakes of black and white in their deathbeds
That's how she reflects, that's how she fights
She displays her flag of courage
Before the billion innocents' eyes.

Caroline Nazareno-Gabis

Biography of a Spirit

The Nile sculpts breathing hieroglyphs in your lips
Great rivers of strength
Flowing, dancing, speaking,
Through your veins,
Your dominance incarnates Existence
Circulating stargates from skylines
Of life and afterlife like waterfall of pilgrims.

Breath by breath, you are the breath of the breathless!
You are the circle of flames of BE-ingness,
The name of complete unimagined wonder
Wandering from Cleopatra's light years,
Your boundless Earth-Sky reveals power for the powerless,
You color the ascending verses
And descending verbs of the universe,
You're the mirror of Reflection
The humming odes behind   maquillage on every face of
     youth,
The ageless epic of your language, the ONE true gift . . .
The Poetry of Life.

Your heart's emblem is a sacred epicene
That glows from the Milky Way of your eyes,
You, a resonating home of selfless heir of heroines
Giving Light to Cimmerian shade of beginnings,
The hallmark of a story within the stories of YOU.

Velvet Passions of Calibrated Quarks

Nirvana in Your Rainbow

I've been to your rainbows,
I starve to be lost in there,
Again . . .
I was bemused by your spectrum,
Which gave me arch to bleed,
With you I drowned,
In the psychedelic sea
Of your metaphysical glimpses.
After the rain,
I am looped in a waterhole,
I stopped. I saw you in my sky,
You become my instant favorite;
Refractions reached me,
I began missing you,
So suddenly.
I stretched my arms,
In a golden pot of silence,
I knew how thousand scarce,
I was; in your twenty-four-hour absence,
And how zillions of nirvanas
You've brought me,
When you kissed me,
At the rainbow's end.

Caroline Nazareno-Gabis

Interstice

i am anywhere
in the crevices
of unknown,
spaces between us,
are spatial mess, upturn dreams.

i am the host of outnumbered filaments
in the wormholes of rummages
that share spots of destiny,
in our certainty shadows,
untold gems of tomorrow.

i am a step towards the line,
devoured centillion dots of bends
while harmonic waves
come to your ears,
as you listen deeply.

i become the center of galaxies
because you radiate interstellar bridges
oscillating equidistant spiral arms,
yes, memories linger
in my gravitational insanity.

Velvet Passions of Calibrated Quarks

Whipping Prophesy

You can find sanguine purveyors
Vitriolic homme d' affaires,
In a rebranded city of diverse riddles
Amidst the congestion of pedicab, dyip and kalesa,
Somehow anointed by fly-by-night mecca,
of exclusive and elusive deals,
of processed or unprocessed dilemma,
Where the great divide takes place,
Forewarned street and sidewalk vendors,
And choked itinerants.
Some are standoff, soon deadlock,
Some have nothing to lose
Because they are protected
By the wards and feudal barons;
While others cryptically float,
Like the Shoal and the fishermen
In caducity.

Caroline Nazareno-Gabis

Mother, There's No Other
In memory and in honor of mothers of the world

Again, why mother?
Mother of Mother's Day,
Mother of a child,
Mother of the unborn,
Mother of angels,
Mother of stolen,
Mother of how many?
Progenitor of love and life.
I realized, I can make a syllabus
for the Subjects to be taught,
I can make the agenda for the meeting,
I can write my to-do list day after day,
Would million of coupon bonds be enough
to write the most fitting, desirable tribute for her?
Or the 10 by 15 feet affiche to announce to the world,
She is valued every Mother's Day.
Give her healing kinesics: A hug, a kiss
after the daybreak, after the laundry,
After work, after all her pains . . .
How far you can hold life's predicaments,
Without HER.

Velvet Passions of Calibrated Quarks

The Verge

let the tumbleweeds
of Renaissance break off
in any way the wind blows,
beyond the horizon,
tantamount to the multidimensional Consciousness.
let the fractals
seize every inch of gestalt canvas,
to manifest reflections
of then and now,
of here, there and everywhere
beyond the numbers.
let the mnemonics of archetypal breakthroughs
in our unembellished Reality,
uncover the unspoken languages
between mankind, nature and other creations.
let the tenets of beauty
flaunt in grace, in harmony, in truth . . .
the bedrock of all colors,
within the pores and anthems of Oneness,
the nexus of masterpieces in Us.

Caroline Nazareno-Gabis

River of Golden Intaglio

Watch my return . . .
Here's the marker of hope,
Mezzotints between the mouth of spring and roots of
    fall . . .
the once running rivers in my palms
yielding flagellations of reality turned into sewerage,
of darkened jade and wizened faces,
untiringly, waiting for halcyon days
where you-me become renewed and recalibrated
why you-me are collisions of aurora borealis in the poles of
    apotheosis,
guided by sacred sanctity: sound, time and geometry
my flowers of life, afterlife
will never wither but transform
the you-me kintsukuroi . . .
no matter losses prick,
no matter pains bend,
no matter fears break,
no matter ruptures mess,
the you-me destiny
are irreplaceable golden mends
in the multiverse.

*Kintsukuroi. ("golden mend") is the Japanese art of mending broken pottery using lacquer resin laced with gold or silver.

Velvet Passions of Calibrated Quarks

soon-to-be-sun poetry

i want my poetry to become exoplanets,
so it can create worlds beyond our systems,
far from vengeance, far from hatred;
it will be a habitable zone of infinite verses,
with or without Kepler telescope,
one poetry shows the same face,
of enormous, sun-like love.

i want my poetry to reach 51 Pegasi b,
the wobbling sun-like star, so close to the parent star,
there will be no distances, no separation,
that it will offer a Great Square of Pegasus,
connecting all hearts to our reborn Earth Sky,
all poetry will be brimming
one reflection that become part of you.

i want my poetry to live
in all walks of life,
recreate and live again,
through the mazes of humanity,
if it needs to walk alone
and find the planets beyond the walls,
let the sun-self crown you wonders,
the haven of a beautiful soul.

Caroline Nazareno-Gabis

Euphoria 10.16.17
For Uno

For today, you can see his tiny fingers
So gently closed,
His ivory scented, milky white socks
Invite tender loving care . . .
The first day we meet,
You are asleep, as we welcome you home,
You're in the arms of your loving Grandma
as I lift the big umbrella,
you become the center of the universe;
Those chinky little eyes
are like reviving innocent crepuscular rays,
and when I see your face,
it carries brimming galaxies.

Velvet Passions of Calibrated Quarks

Wish

I want the carolers sing for the nymphs,
gather all children
to meet Sophia the humanoid,
who smiles with her rubber skin,
who speaks with conversational artificial intelligence,
then ask Santa Claus, do something for my wish,
more Sophias to clean the city,
save people from disasters,
escape extra judicial killings,
freeze the avalanche of the youths' dreams.
I want to ride the sleigh,
solve thousands of reindeers' paces,
from the North Pole,
where gazillions of festive pops
and bags for souls,
return in frosty ballads,
to recreate wreaths
of believing.

Caroline Nazareno-Gabis

Devi's Mundial De Tango
Superstar's Dance

Shine on Superstar!
Her ensembles freeing, tattooing the night life,
Chandeliers ramp from sandstorms' wishful veranda,
Bring her shoes inside the artisan's dance floor,
Sweet, genuine sometimes rough stares,
Herculean way of dressing un-abandoned majesty,
In cadence, betraying the morbid swooping jazz,
Counter-clockwise trance, beguiling glance on the faraway
    lodge.
Gaelic damsel's caveat, from Rumi's pledge of serenity,
To Sufi's astral-fractal-sparkling-notes shaping minds,
Her Picasso hands swirling rainbow inception as she
    tiptoes . . .
One, two, three. Perhaps unuttered sublime soliloquy,
Visage of poetry wandering ordeals of connected souls,
Just before the Bhurj Kalifa's celestial lawn.
Her warmth, her verve, her brilliance, her undefying
    laurels,
Born as the centerpiece and the masterpiece . . .
Within her creativity is the language spoken
Humanity's festivity – overflowing perfumes of goodwill
The oracles of messengers beyond the helm,
Sashaying woven steps in the hearts of men.

Velvet Passions of Calibrated Quarks

The Song My Heart Sings

You came along
just like the sun facing the earth
spreading its light,
the sunrise that melts,
the icebergs that freeze my heart.

You passed by
just like a firework in the ethereal space
leaving fluorescence,
sparkling in a wide room,
that defines the eyes of love.

You stood unmoved
just like a monolith, stone for ages,
building the monuments of your un-fleeting words,
the luster that heals,
the faults and withered
part of life.

And if my heart finds the perfect rhythm
you'll be my voice, my endless song.

Caroline Nazareno-Gabis

Euphoric Diffusion

When the air gently kisses
and piercing my cheeks,
i remember your scent,

When the bed
takes me to velvety,
warm, sheltered metaphors,
and put me into spaces
of no surrenders,
it is you,
traversing
in the streams of my being.

When the moon sighs
to the stars,
whispering goodnight wishes,
it is you and me,
suffuse in trance,
on our first honeymoon dance.

Velvet Passions of Calibrated Quarks

where peace can be

million years of ifs and buts
eloquently circulating in many tongues
crossroads of meanings read aloud
but found meaningless . . .
unheard unseen unrealized.

should it just be a theme to write about?
a blockbuster movie to queue up
should i play the role
of a gladiator
a hero
a warrior
a prize fighter
a soldier?

and broadcast a nation address
"now is the total absence"
of combats, of chaos, and bloodshed
does it mean safe and sound?
when my brothers are homeless and dead?

always been a missing piece
it's nowhere.
the ceasefire
is in the heart
of human race.

Caroline Nazareno-Gabis

Waltz with the Rain Princess

See me in the crystal drops
Falling from the celestial throne,
Meet me inside the cooling cloudburst sound,
And I will sing to you
The sonatas of the mountains, the rivers and the lakes
In our free willing autumn carpet,
As it bids the grand Sol,
Capturing my pacified retina.
I will take you with me
In our muddy floors,
Where we'll dance our first waltz,
Together, like Zeus and Hera.
All the wonders we'll breathe
Let us teach our feet the tiptoes of happiness
Then wrap me with your arms,
All days, all nights, always . . .
Like countless raindrops,
Only this muted umbrella
Can witness our castle built with kisses,
In our royal waltz under the rain.

Velvet Passions of Calibrated Quarks

Sequester X

Holding no legal papers
For the birth of a rational mind,
No hierarchy
Of purity of hearts.
No marks of lame, blame or fame
Of big and small, mucho and nothing.
No payments
For selfless love expressed,
No extra charges
For the soul of sacrifice.
I am the name
The purpose, the lifeblood
Of my character.
Conceiving a sliver
Of compassion,
No genus of genetic codes
To spot and scour insensibility,
Indifference is just a recall.
A serenade to remember
For the homeless, for all
One heart at a time.

Caroline Nazareno-Gabis

Nexus in My Canvas

I mount my tripod to break free from paralysis,
Squeeze black holes of cheers to start,
Open the windows where my garden of beauty springs,
Chrysalis of hope keeps knocking in full winged-blooms,
Compassion intrudes to my unseasoned oil paintings
To reckon masterpieces and the longing faces,
I dazzle acrylic touches on the peacocks to spread their
    plumage
To offer colors of love and serve sheer drops of believing,
These sables run to all the starfishes to stamp stars on
    children's palms,
That would be a starry day to welcome the early moonless
    dusk.
Inner voices shake the hourglass of plains and plateaus
To sift borderless colorless weightless mercy
Together we can build the Empire State of our dreams,
Spawning coral parachutes from the ocean floors of
    goodwill,
I rub balms of solace from Atlantis to rain extra care to all
    Nature friends,
My fervent request for an assemblage of tamed gargoyles
To connect with the young ones even the un-hatched little
    darlings.
Teach them that the heart has more rooms to give,
Without cage of fear, without distrust, without trembles,
With this palette I weld rainbow bridges so everybody can
    come and sing
Reasons to live, chances to dance as Sister Morning shines
Mirrors of sunny semblance to vivify over and over again,
I infuse skylarks with healing snowflakes and Siberian
    wind to pack kisses . . .
For every tiny, every huge creature in this living canvas
I feel and touch without texture quarantines,
I rise from this vessel of a reborn self; I paint allies of
    wisdom,

Velvet Passions of Calibrated Quarks

Raise all flags of smiles, wave written whispering wishes
Of unsung wonders from today to the future, and beyond
    tomorrow's birth;
Withstand the tears of meltdown, embrace the canopy of
    brand new leaves of beginning.
Build castles of doubtless reigns, sanctuaries of emerging
    cinders to tribunes of strength,
Here-there-everywhere reside the real unforgotten core,
Deep-rooted Threshold of the Never Lost.

Caroline Nazareno-Gabis

Meraki

every craft, piece by piece
hovering ripened species of passion,
refined apocalyptic rendition
breathing covenant of spaces and aces,
like mosaics of mountain-dream-capsules wrapped in
    Tibetan dews,
wreaths of purple hyacinths under the jade moonlight,
our bosom of oceanic waterfalls,
become offspring of our memories.

every piece of Mason jars
devoted to your lips
drinking crystalline creativity,
where star folks' manna pours
anointing flame from Urduja's waterbed of time
restores the Pi's salt to sprinkle prismatic utters;
in your heart is a bedrock of depth, balance, and wellspring,
our saved lanterns of pomegranate lullabies,
devouring wanderlust's loops of treasured diamonds,
hybrids of men, women and children,
the unframed melodies of reality.

every fruition of ends and beginnings,
every sweet ruins of nothingness,
every rising every time we fall,
every morning where reigning glorious sun
resides in us; the wonders and miracles
the beautiful celebration, gift of life.

  (4TH Place, World Union of Poets Poetry Prize 2016)

*meraki [may-rah-kee] (adjective) is a word that modern Greeks often use to describe doing something with; merakiul, creativity, or love: when you put "something of yourself" into what you're doing, whatever it may be.

Velvet Passions of Calibrated Quarks

Call Me Cypher

I walk along the way
like a zilch under a fig tree
there is a moment of clarity
as i hatch the eggs
of sundry loose ends.

I talk once and maybe more
out of the machines
running wild inside
my remaining veins.

How can i be smaller
when i drive to Sin City?
how can i be bigger
when i share a heart for free?
how can i be a grinch
when i utter the rots and clots
of my angry throat?
how can i be beautiful
when i see all like squares?
how can i be enough
when i fill others'
empty bottles?
how much numbers can tell
if i have no one; but myself?

Caroline Nazareno-Gabis

Bedazzled

in the morning i am sipping
all the calmness of your voice,
i own the multitude of dreams,
the solace of northern skies
haunting my soul,
the glow in your eyes
were the total recall
wincing me love.

i walk my days on a shore,
my footprints and yours
are one,
at time you wait for the answer
i love you
my sweet surrender.

Velvet Passions of Calibrated Quarks

because i can be

the morning mist to quench you,
your days, your nights,
feel those tiny drops
to refresh your mind,
your soul, your being,
each moment reminds me,
you're all i have.

the air in your lungs
the breath you take
in and out,
the sound of life
while i spread my wings
to fly with you,
to walk every step,
 save those footprints
and take me to the highways
of becoming.

the sky, the clouds
the new moon, the haze
the rainbow and the sun
sharing all the hues
and colors of life,
and for life.
the landscapes of my soul
from you.

i will stay in the dust
to take you a part of me,
i will be in the tornadoes' eyes
no matter how cruel,
i will be there,
i will be in you,
in my before and after glow.

Caroline Nazareno-Gabis

anywhere, everywhere
as time travels
to many shapes and distances,
in many ways,
in many hours,
in many chances,
because i can be all,
the reflection of my all,
because i am in you.

Velvet Passions of Calibrated Quarks

I See No Other from Yesterday

i am jenny,
hopping freely from canopy of canticles,
watching seagulls by the seashore,
humming like robins
after the storms and thunders,
stepping on the board-way
of this apex without borders.
i listen to Minerva
dispersing her thoughts,
from psalms of our reigning universe,
up these stairs and scaffoldings,
i asked for the bottom-line,
of no others, of no outcast
of our own time.
uplifting the quagmire
of unreachable, and impossible,
i toss the coin
and hold on;
i am beyond the valleys of possibilities,
stride my glides,
in our lighthouse of unforgotten
ordinary things,
we smile,
we knit,
we fondle
TOGETHER.

Caroline Nazareno-Gabis

Pandora escapes unto my hands

time exists in my hands
as dreams escalate to wilderness,
born from the ages of prodigy
where wordsmith come,
in the breathing dawn
to the free cycles
of wind
of water
of fire
saving the hourglass of all-giving
on the day
i become
a reality.

Velvet Passions of Calibrated Quarks

Godiva and the Music

Do you still remember
how to play the music
of getting up,
wave the mettle in sync
to be the one,
the better one?

Do you still remember
the fading faces of time,
underneath
the swallowing perfection,
off-the-wall
unveiling
their sapphire kingdom
but no one
returns?

Do you still remember
the time you fell
from the death bed
of surrenders,
yet again and again,
your knees flex and stretch
to sketch another
clear sky?

Caroline Nazareno-Gabis

Epilogue

about the Author

Caroline 'Ceri Naz' Nazareno-Gabis, World Poetry Canada International Director to The Philippines, is a multi-awarded contemporary poet, editor, journalist, educator, peace and women's advocate.

Caroline graduated cum laude with the degree of Bachelor of Elementary Education, specialized in General Science at the Pangasinan State University-Bayambang, Ceri Naz has been a voracious researcher in various arts, science and literature. She volunteered in Richmond Multicultural Concerns Society, TELUS World Science, Vancouver Art Gallery, and Vancouver Aquarium. She also experiments on deviantArt, mask- and shell-painting, and collecting artworks from the exquisite nature. Her photo-art, "koireography", was exhibited in South Korea, with the theme "VISIBLE POETRY CONNECTING THE WORLD". Her mentor in photography is her husband, Bryann, a freelance photographer and a professional teacher. As a science educator, she founded the American Society for Rickettsiology at the University of Montana – her research niche on biological safety.

The author's prestigious poetic belts include the place of the 7th Prize Winner in the 19th and 20th Award International Cultural Festival (Italy); Writers International Network-Canada's "Amazing Poet 2015", The Frang Bardhi Literary Prize 2014

(Albania), the Şair-Gazeteci or Poet-Journalist Award 2014 (Tuzla, Istanbul, Turkey), World Poetry Empowered Poet 2013 (Vancouver, Canada), and World Poetry Canada Poet Piper 2012.

Caroline Nazareno-Gabis' creative writings have been published in various anthologies worldwide. She also served as one of the juries of local and international writing competitions like Commaful's Next Top Writer, Poets in Nigeria and more.

The author is a Member of World Academy of Arts and Culture, Chief Advisor to the President of the World Nations Writers' Union in Kazakhstan on Contemporary World Literature, Honorary Member of World Higher Literary Academic Council of World Nations' Writers Union, featured member of Association of Women's Rights and Development (AWID), Member of the Advisory Board of ATUNIS Galaktika Poetike, Asia Pacific Writers and Translators (APWT), The Poetry Posse, Axlepino and Anacbanua.

Beyond her literary endeavour, Caroline Nazareno-Gabis teaches Science, Technology and Society, Environmental Science, General Biology, Organic Chemistry and General Chemistry at the Tarlac Agricultural University in The Philippines. She was a scholar of Environmental Genomics with the Indian Technical and Economic Cooperation (ITEC) Programme in 2018.

Author's Links

apwriters.org/author/ceri_naz/

www.thewonderwomenworld.com/?p=3925&fbclid=IwAR2ztDKGFN09Qo7afzAb_dGukJwsKaBtijsPO8fGvqO08apE1voBtpDN8Lk

www.milesdepoemas.cl/carolinenazareno.htm

www.manilatimes.net/three-poems-5/319110/

www.wnwu.org/index.php/en/our-members/186-chief-advisor-to-the-president-of-the-world-nations-writars-union-in-kazakhstan-on-contemporary-world-literature

panitikan.ph/category/authors/page/2/

Inner Child Press

Inner Child Press is a publishing company founded and operated by writers. Our personal publishing experiences provide us an intimate understanding of the sometimes-daunting challenges writers, new and seasoned, may face in the business of publishing and marketing their creative "Written Work".

For more information:

Inner Child Press

www.innerchildpress.com
intouch@innerchildpress.com

'building bridges of cultural understanding'

www.innerchildpress.com

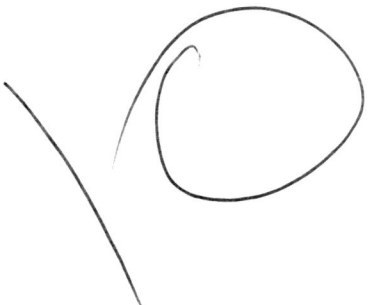

Premier alphabet français divisé par syllabes : apprendre aux enfants a épeler avec facilité (Éd. 1853)